FROM PUBLIC SERVICE TO PRIVATE SECTOR

ESSENTIAL QUESTIONS TO CONSIDER AS YOU
TRANSITION TO GOVERNMENT CONTRACTOR

Danielle O. Saunders

FROM PUBLIC SERVICE TO PRIVATE SECTOR

ESSENTIAL QUESTIONS TO CONSIDER AS YOU TRANSITION TO GOVERNMENT CONTRACTOR

ISBN: 978-0-615-35589-4

1350 Beverly Road

Suite 115

PMB 220

McLean, Virginia 22101-3633

www.transitionpublishing.net

e-mail: info@transitionpublishing.net

Please contact us about volume purchase discounts.

INTRODUCTION

Congratulations on entering this next phase of your professional career!

Since establishing my own government contracting firm in 2006, I have had the pleasure of meeting and interviewing hundreds of people, just like you, who are embarking on the transition from government employee to government contractor. I know from my interactions with those individuals that this decision is not without mixed emotion.

I wrote this book so I could share with you the experiences that I have had assisting those embarking on the same journey with making the career decision which is right for them—personally, professionally, and financially. I found that many people looking to make this transition do not focus on the right issues and thus do not receive all of the available data that they should consider to make the most fully informed decision.

I use the term "career decision" intentionally because the primary focus of this book is to assist those who are looking for a longer term career opportunity and not just a job. However, even for those not necessarily looking for a long-term career, the information in this book will give you situational awareness and allow you to make the process work to your advantage. The government's need for professionals with the requisite skills, experience, understanding of mission requirements, and clearance levels far exceeds the currently available supply of such talent. The opportunities are certainly there—it's up to you to make the most of them.

Finding a job is a matter of time, while identifying a career opportunity requires a more focused and proactive effort. This book contains those issues and questions which should be considered as you evaluate your professional opportunities. Some of the issues might not be important to you—and that is fine. It is just imperative that you at least consider each issue and dismiss it, rather than not give it any thought and make a decision which may not ultimately be the best decision for you over the long term.

I also should note that I am an attorney by training and have practiced in the private sector for twenty years in the areas of corporate organization, employment and public and private finance. This book is not intended to give legal advice but rather to give you an awareness of some of the relevant potential issues and practical resolutions for consideration.

Finally, and most importantly, I want to thank you for your public service and wish you every success in your transition to the private sector. If you have any questions or comments, I would be delighted to hear from you. Please e-mail me at dsaunders@ transitionpublishing.net.

Danielle O. Saunders

FORWARD

Ms. Saunders has prepared a concise and informative book that will aid people in transitioning successfully from public service to private sector employment. It is important that individuals in career transition who are seeking rewarding employment opportunities with private companies understand the differences in the two employment sectors if they are to be successful in their new endeavors in private industry. Most retiring employees need first to become familiar with the private sector's vocabulary, which is different from government-speak, and this book addresses this often-confusing topic.

Those changing to an industrial contractor position with the government will first be employees of a private company that will have its own set of requirements and expectations that are separate from their government contract responsibilities. By carefully reading Ms. Saunders's book, transitioning government employees will become familiar with the several differing employers' expectations they will encounter while seeking employment among the companies in this area.

One of the most important areas Ms. Saunders covers is the necessity for those in transition to understand that in the private sector, employees themselves must be the driving force in their career decisions. As such, they should not simply be pliable assets that a company assigns to a position because it is convenient for the company. Retirees will find helpful her advice that it is essential that retiring people decide what they want to do for the remainder of their working life, before they have interviews. As she points out, only then will they be able to intelligently make decisions regarding which company they should join. Whether you are retiring after a full career of public service or looking for a change mid-career, after you read her book, you will not sell yourself short.

Frederick A. Turco, retired from public service and currently working in the private sector.

"With a little time and a proactive effort on your part, you can find an opportunity which meets both your personal and professional objectives."

CONTENTS

Introduction 3

Forward 5

FROM PUBLIC SERVICE TO THE PRIVATE SECTOR

ESSENTIAL QUESTIONS TO CONSIDER AS YOU
TRANSITION TO GOVERNMENT CONTRACTOR

1. How is Government Contracting different in the
    private sector? 8

2. What do You want to do?.................................10

3. Are you getting hired for a particular position or as
    a Professional? 14

4. What about Compensation? 16

5. How do you evaluate Equity Components of
    compensation?.. 19

6. What about being an Independent Consultant? 22

7. Any Final Tips for successful transitioning?................... 24

ANNEX 1 – Most Common Reasons people leave their
employer company 26

ANNEX 2 – Forms of Non-Salary Compensation.................... 28

QUESTION 1
HOW IS GOVERNMENT CONTRACTING DIFFERENT IN THE PRIVATE SECTOR?

Government Contracting is a very unique industry. Unlike workers in most other industries, professionals in government contracting typically spend more time with their government clients than they do with the people in the company for whom they work. Frequently, government contractors report to work at their customer's site and do not spend much time at their company's offices. This separation often leads people to focus on and identify with their contract position while not giving much consideration to their actual employer.

When I ask contractors where they work, more than half will respond with the name of the group within the government for whom they perform services. Most do not respond with the name of their actual employer, Company X. As a result, people often underestimate the amount of support and the underlying connection which they should be receiving from their company. Your employer should be providing you with more than just a paycheck—but you need to know what you have a right to expect, and then you need to ask for it.

You and your employer should be in a long term partnership—together. I am not advocating that you should be making a decision to stay with your new private employer for the rest of your professional life, but, as you know (or are about to experience), the quest for a new employer is very time consuming and can be emotionally taxing. Decisions should be made carefully and deliberately to avoid mistakes.

Another unique aspect of the government contracting industry is that most competing companies often wind up working together as teammates. It is not uncommon to see contractors from numerous different companies working in the same government office on the same program. You will want to keep this in mind as you go through the interviewing process because you may decide you do not wish to work directly for a particular company, but you may wind up working indirectly for the same company on one of its programs. The world of government contractors is indeed a small one.

QUESTION 2
WHAT DO YOU WANT TO DO?

While this may seem like a basic, fundamental question, it consistently seems to be the most difficult question for former government employees to answer. Typically, in the government organizational structure, people are rarely asked what they would like to do, but instead people are simply told where their contributions are needed. Consequently, it is not instinctive or natural for those same people to take an entirely different and more proactive approach and to consider what it is they would find most personally rewarding in this next phase of their professional lives.

This question of deciding what is best for you becomes more challenging when the majority of government contractors grow their employee base in response to newly awarded or expanded projects and recruit directly against the needs of that particular project. If you are speaking to Company X at a time when its new project requires it to provide analytical support, for example, you can be certain that the focus of your conversations with this company will be your analytical experience. If Company X has unfilled analytical positions, it is losing money (revenue) each day that those positions remain vacant, and your personal desires in terms of skill or focus may be secondary to their objectives.

In my experience, people who have spent time in government service have had a multitude of different opportunities and have had the good fortune to work in different parts of their particular organization. (This variety of experience does not generally occur to such extent in the private sector). As a result, people coming from the government have much more experience and are qualified to do many more things than they actually believe. Unfortunately, they don't often discuss these possibilities with their potential new employers and instead focus on the currently available opportunity.

When most people interview with me, they tell me that they have heard that I have a great company and they are interested in becoming a part of it. They then ask me what positions I have open or what specific project requirements I am trying to fill. You easily can see how this would now limit the discussion to the company's immediate needs.

In early meetings with potential candidates, immediate needs are rarely discussed. The better strategy instead is to understand what particular people enjoy doing and what they will find challenging and rewarding at this particular point in their professional career so that they are excited to go to work and serve the customer in their new role as government contractors.

The increasingly complex needs of the government are not going to be met solely by contractors who are filling open requirements for eight hours each day at the behest of their employer, but rather by professionals who have the requisite skills and experience along with the desire to help the government solve ever-evolving challenges. When people are doing what they genuinely and passionately enjoy doing, amazing successes happen.

Many colleagues at my firm had impressive accomplishments and successes in government service and very distinguished careers. In my eyes, they are truly American heroes. So, what does a professional like that do for an encore as a contractor? It should be the responsibility of a company to bring out the best in its employees and to position them for success—and that will occur when the company takes the time to understand all facets of a potential employee's career, along with the experiences which that person found most rewarding. Hiring against a particular position and limiting discussions to that position may not always achieve the desired long-term results.

Some people transitioning from government service also are eager to learn the business of the government contracting industry as well as continuing to serve government customers. However, with most government contractors, there is a clear distinction between those working in the corporate office and those on client contracts and the two paths seldom cross unless a deliberate attempt is made on the part of both the company and the employee.

Things to Consider When Interviewing for a Contractor Position:

√ When putting together your resume, don't just list your past positions and accomplishments in reverse chronological order. Instead, give thought to your most rewarding experiences and highlight the skills that enabled you to perform successfully in those situations. Continue to emphasize those same skills and illustrate how the skills were used in prior roles.

√ Create an objective section at the beginning of your resume and emphasize clearly what you would like to be doing in this next phase of your professional career. Keep in mind that there is no "standard" or "required" format for a resume in connection with an interview with a potential company employer. Note that some government programs may require that candidate resumes be submitted for approval in a specified format, but that exercise should occur only after you have made the independent decision to join the company—because of its culture, core values and breadth of available professional opportunities—and not solely for that particular program.

√ In early discussions, don't spend too much time engaging about specific positions. Instead, focus the conversation on some of the issues highlighted in the next sections of this book. It is not uncommon to have more than one interview with the same company prior to making a decision. In fact, I met with each of the key members of my senior management team at least three times following their retirement from government service and their decision to accept my offer of employment.

√ If you are also interested in learning the business side of government contracting, it is important to understand the backgrounds of the people for whom you will be working and who are charged with management of the organization. Do they have experience in the business world or are they retired public servants and is this their first foray into the private sector? The answer is important as it will have a direct impact on the experience you will have in this company, especially if one of your goals is to learn the business of the government contracting business.

√ Focus discussions on what you enjoy doing professionally. Think about the skills you needed to utilize to make past experiences rewarding. If you enjoy instructing, then lead with that. It doesn't matter that your last instructional position was not the most recent. Equally as important, clearly communicate what you don't want to be doing at this point in your career. I have interviewed many former government employees who tell me that they have no desire to travel any more. I also have met many people who do not want to perform services as a contractor for their former office. Instead, they are looking for an opportunity to apply their skills and experiences to solve challenges in a different environment. They are looking for more than a "do over" in their former organization. Also note that, by law, contractors cannot have the same authority which they enjoyed as government employees. For some, this has proved very disappointing and led to an employment change shortly after transition.

√ Don't compromise your personal objectives. Life is too short and you will regret the decision. If you want to work only part time, be clear and definitive with any potential employer. In my firm, almost 10% of my colleagues work less than full time because they have other things they also want to focus on at this stage of their life. There are plenty of opportunities for part-time employment. Of course, for an employer, the same amount of time is required to recruit and hire a part-time employee as a full time one, so most will try to persuade candidates to work full time, at least early on. Also, don't consider a longer commute than you believe is personally acceptable. With a little time and a proactive effort on your part, you can find an opportunity which meets both your personal and professional objectives.

QUESTION 3
ARE YOU GETTING HIRED FOR A PARTICULAR POSITION OR AS A PROFESSIONAL TO BE PART OF AN ORGANIZATION?

One of the most important elements in your employment decision is to have a clear understanding as to whether the company is hiring you for a particular position or to become a member of the company's team. It is clear to me from interviewing many people who were looking to change employers that they did not have clarity on this important question when they made the earlier employment decision.

When a company hires someone to join the team, there is an implicit understanding that the person is being looked at in a broader sense, as a professional, for all of their skills, experiences and potential, and not just for an immediate open position. A company that is hiring someone to join the team is also making a bigger commitment in terms of support and sometimes training to give the person all of the tools needed to be successful. Also, the company is giving the person the opportunity to apply previous skills to new challenges and to continue to learn and grow professionally. Employees from these sorts of companies relate more to the company with which they are employed and do not tend to identify themselves with the function or position in which they are currently performing.

To determine whether you are being considered as a professional or being hired for a particular position, ask the following questions:

√ What is the company's policy if a contract or program position ends? Will my employment be terminated after a stated period of time?

✓ What resources are available to assist me in identifying and evaluating other client work?

✓ Is there an opportunity for me to work in the corporate office for some period of time (assuming that is of interest)?

✓ Will the company keep me informed of other opportunities which may be appealing to me? If so, how are those opportunities communicated?

✓ What is the process if I would like to change my client work? Must I stay in a position for a specified time? Is it my responsibility to identify a replacement for me before I can move to another project?

✓ Does the company permit working on more than one client program simultaneously? If so, how is that handled?

✓ Is there an opportunity for me to get on a management track? If so, what is the process and how can I become eligible?

QUESTION 4
WHAT ABOUT COMPENSATION?

Compensation always seems to be a challenging issue—for a variety of reasons. Some people have a very clear idea of the compensation they are looking to earn in the private sector, sometimes without the knowledge or experience to consider all facets of a particular situation (such as the contract rate, the company's salary scale, other non-salary compensation (see Annex 2), etc.). Often, these people do not make the best career decision for themselves because their main focus is salary, and they will select an employer based on who will pay them the salary they have in their head—then end up working on a client project which may not be inspiring or rewarding for them. Other people go through the process with no idea as to what they should ask for in terms of compensation. They may know what they want to do in terms of work, but haven't given any thought to their new market value.

Let me share with you some realities in terms of government contractor compensation:

√ Every company is unique in terms of compensation packages. This is because each company has its own individual benefits and compensation plan. While two companies may offer the very same base salary, the overall aggregate compensation could vary by as much as 50% when you take into account the total package. Some companies pay a base salary regardless of how many hours are worked and others specify a base salary and pay based on actual hours worked. For those of you who travel and tend to work overtime, you can see how this could create a disparity. Make sure you take the time to understand the details.

√ Benefits are compensation. You must take into account the value of all of the benefits being offered as well as salary to be in a position to make an accurate comparison. Most companies can itemize the value of each of the benefits offered (I know mine can) but it is always surprising how many times we don't share that information—because people don't ask for it. If there are benefits offered which are not important to you, you can ask if there is something else you can receive instead. Some companies offer "cafeteria type" benefit plans where you will be allotted a certain amount of cash value to "purchase" benefits. If none or not all of the benefits are purchased, you receive cash which is taxable as additional compensation.

√ When valuing the amount of tax deferred compensation (profit-sharing or an employer 401(k) contribution), remember to include the tax deferral benefit as well as the actual amount of the contribution in your calculation of value. For some, this could be significant.

√ If you are joining a company with the intention to work primarily on a client project, the salary you will receive must be sustainable, i.e. consistent with the payment the company will receive for performance of your services on that particular project. I know this sounds simple, but many people don't understand why they can't earn more than X dollars on project Y. It is highly unusual for a company to take a loss on an employee—unless of course you are a publicly recognized expert in your field, in which case a company may pay a premium for the cache of having you on the team.

If you follow the guidance recommended in Section 7, Any Final Tips for a Successful Transition?, you should be able to get an understanding of the acceptable salary range for any position you may be considering.

√ At the end of the day, even though government contracting firms are serving the public sector, they have to be profitable to stay in business. There are well known industry standards for measuring financial results of government contracting firms, such as EBITDA (earnings before interest, taxes, depreciation and amortization— also known as earnings or sometimes generally referred to as profit), contribution per employee (the amount of revenue generated by an employee in excess of his or her direct labor cost and benefits), and wrap rate (the rate by which you multiply direct labor to determine revenue). A well-run and financially sound company will strive to stay within an acceptable range of these metrics with all new hires. I would be quite worried and a bit hesitant to join any firm which didn't make compensation decisions in this manner.

QUESTION 5
HOW DO YOU EVALUATE EQUITY COMPONENTS OF COMPENSATION?

A few companies in the government contracting industry offer some form of equity (either direct or in the form of options) as part of their compensation package. However, it is critical to understand the basics of how equity compensation works in order to evaluate this benefit in the decision-making process. And, just like companies themselves, an offer of equity type compensation can come in many different forms.

The following are the most common forms of equity type compensation and related issues for consideration:

√ Publicly-traded companies have a known market value and may offer key employees stock options or the right to purchase company stock at a discount to market price pursuant to an employee stock purchase plan. In either case, the value of the benefit can be determined at the time of the grant and can be measured subsequently. Participation in a stock purchase plan would allow you to purchase public company stock at a discount to the price at which you could buy the same stock in the public markets. The typical discount ranges from 5 -15%. For any significant benefit to be realized, the company must continue to perform well so the stock will hold or increase its value. The amount of taxation on any gain will depend on the length of time the stock is held after purchase. Note that an actual cash investment is required as part of this type of plan and there may be some restrictions on the re-sale of this stock in the public markets.

Public companies often also have stock option plans. An option is the right to purchase equity at some point in the future at today's market value (or a discount thereto). Options are also sometimes used as retention tools as the right to purchase the equity may actually vest over a set number of years (typically 3-5 years). Unlike with a stock purchase plan, with an option, you do not have to invest in the company first (and thus be out of pocket) to realize a gain down the road. It is also important to know whether your company's stock option plan is an "incentive stock option plan" or a "non-qualified plan" as you may experience a tax event at the time of an initial grant or upon exercise of the option.

These tax implications should be discussed with your personal tax advisor. Also, you should ask to see the plan documentation (for either an option or stock purchase plan) prior to making any decision as to the value you will place on this component of compensation.

√ Private companies (both large and small) also may offer some type of stock compensation or equity participation. The major difference in this case is that there is no readily ascertainable market value of privately held equity. There are a variety of industry accepted formulas which can be used to estimate value, but there is no established market value until the time that someone actually makes an offer to purchase the company—and that then becomes the market value.

Additionally, unlike with public companies, there is no ready market for stock in a privately held company and this makes the investment or benefit completely illiquid. If you receive equity (either stock or options) in a privately held company, you may not realize any liquidity unless and until the owner(s) decide to sell all or part of the company. So if you are considering equity as a portion of compensation as you compare opportunities, make sure you understand the business plan and exit strategy of the company so you can properly assess the value of this benefit. Also, there may be significant tax consequences to an equity or option grant depending on how the grant is made and whether or not it is made pursuant to a plan. Ask to see the plan documentation in advance and inquire about who will assume any tax liability before making any decisions.

I have met many people who have made career decisions based on the promise of equity value and who have ended up very disappointed. In some cases, a liquidity timeframe was promised and then the owner(s) decided not to sell the company. Many of these people went out of pocket to invest in the company (by exercising their options and paying the purchase price to buy stock) and have no idea if or when they will see their investment returned or realize any gain. Other people were granted what they perceived to be on its face a very large number of stock options (5,000 for example).

However, they did not know at the time they were allured by this option grant that certain other information and metrics would need to be known in order to determine the value. For example, if they were granted 5,000 stock options, they might not know the amount of the total authorized or the total issued shares to determine the percentage of company ownership which they had received. They also did not understand dilution, i.e. the fact that their ownership interest in terms of a percentage may decrease over time with each additional grant.

These examples are by no means meant to discourage you from becoming excited about or accepting equity as part of a compensation package. Rather, they illustrate the importance of knowing exactly what you are getting so you realistically and accurately can assess this part of the offer and make an informed decision.

QUESTION 6
WHAT ABOUT BEING AN INDEPENDENT CONSULTANT?

Many people who serve as part of the government contracting community do so in the capacity as an independent consultant (also commonly referred to as an independent contractor, an IC or a 1099—the latter term referring to the tax form such person receives in lieu of a W-2) rather than an employee. There is no definitive answer for all situations as the decision to work as an independent consultant should be made by each person individually, taking into account his or her own personal tax situation, compensation requirements, and work preferences. Some agencies within the government are subject to restrictions and may be forced to work only with independent consultants as opposed to working with employees of government contracting companies (also known as industrial contractors). Others can work with both types.

People who work as independent consultants will tell you that they enjoy the flexibility of the work schedule—they can work only when they want to on projects and programs of their own choosing, and they are not subject to company requirements regarding minimum number of hours or other corporate policies and procedures. They also may feel a sense of empowerment because they have more control over their work conditions and do not have to answer to anyone other than their particular client. They usually are paid a straight hourly or per diem rate plus reimbursable expenses. For many, working as an independent consultant is a simple and satisfactory situation.

As an independent consultant, however, you are responsible for your own tax withholdings (and must make estimated tax payments) and you may pay a higher tax rate. You must do your own invoicing and maintain your own corporate entity should you choose to establish one for tax reasons or protecting against liability.

You also do not receive the benefits which are available to employees, such as accrued leave, paid insurance coverage, 401k or other company deferred compensation contributions. These extra benefits can add up!

Independent consultants also are not on any kind of corporate career path nor do they have the opportunity to create any equity value since they are selling only their time. I would advise anyone considering this as a career option to consult with his or her own personal tax advisor before making this decision and to do a thorough comparison of total costs and benefits.

QUESTION 7
ANY FINAL TIPS FOR A SUCCESSFUL TRANSITION?

1.   **TAKE YOUR TIME.** You will find a job if you want one. There are currently not enough candidates with the requisite skills, experience and often level of clearance to meet the government's need for support. So, take your time, ask the questions suggested in this book, and carefully consider the answers you receive. Meet with the companies which interest you more than once, maybe even several times, and meet with more than one representative from the company.

2.   **ASK FOR A WRITTEN OFFER BUT DON'T FEEL PRESSURED TO SIGN BEFORE YOU ARE READY TO COMMIT.** If you ask for a written offer, you will be in a much better position to consider all facets of the opportunity, compare it fairly with other offers and make a fully informed decision. You also will be in a better position to clear up any misunderstandings about how bonuses or other benefits may apply if you can review the terms in writing. While it is perfectly acceptable to sign a contingent offer (which is non-binding) at any time and with multiple companies, don't feel pressured to do so as there can be some downside. Sometimes companies will submit you for a particular position after you have signed a contingent offer but before you have fully committed—and that may preclude subsequent companies from the opportunity to have you work on that same program.

3.   **UNDERSTAND YOUR POSITION.** If you will be working on a specific government contract, take the time to understand the business terms of your particular contract above and beyond the scope of work you will be performing. Some important contract terms which can affect your professional future are:

a) Period of Performance (or term of the contract). Understand how long the performance period is and when it is over.

b) Proposed Level and Rate. Be familiar with the level and rate at which you are starting on a program. Ask about how you can increase your level if warranted by your performance.

c) Annual Contract Escalation. This is the amount of rate increase which the government has agreed to accept during the term of the contract. Many companies base annual salary increases solely on contract escalation. Ask your company about its policy in this regard.

d) Ability to change Labor Categories. If applicable to your particular program, will you have mobility to change labor categories and enhance your compensation once you have experience on the program?

Make sure the offer you receive is sustainable and not just a bait-and-switch to get you to join the company.

4. **BE PROACTIVE.** Since no one has more of a vested interest in your professional career than you do, you need to be the one who is the most forward and proactive in this process. Government contracting firms (especially the large ones) are always looking for experienced professionals with security clearances as the firms have many open positions on any given day of the week—and remember, an unfilled position means lost revenue. They will pursue you and try to get you corralled into their recruitment process where you will pop out at the end and be filling one of these current open positions. (Hence, the nickname "body shops" for some of these companies.) Don't let yourself become a passive participant in their recruiting cycle. Discuss what you want to do and what you are looking for in this new chapter of your professional life. Ask the questions referenced in this book. Remember, many companies serve the same customers on the same programs. Once you identify the kind of work you would like to do, choose your company home wisely.

ANNEX 1

Top 10 Reasons People Tell Me they want to leave their Private Employer Company (They should have read this book before making a private sector decision)

1. The position I was hired for was cancelled or my employer did not win the contract award or re-compete.

2. I have been in the same position for X years and want to change—but no one in my company is helping me identify a new position.

3. I don't feel that my company recognizes me as an individual and I am not given the opportunity to utilize more of my skills. My day-to-day job is repetitive and I don't see any path for professional growth.

4. I have no real connection to my company. I go from my home to my customer site and then back home. I am not plugged into what is going on at my company's corporate office. As a result, I don't feel that I have any role in my company's strategic growth or ultimate success.

5. I am not learning anything new.

6. I accepted a position in the company's corporate office, but I don't feel that the company is giving me the tools to be successful. I want to go back to working directly for government customers since I am comfortable that I know how to do that well.

7. I have some ideas for new solutions for my customers, but no one is interested at my company—and I don't see a way to take the idea forward.

8. My company bosses are asking me to do something (usually travel) that I don't want to do. They told me to do it for a while until they can find a replacement (backfill) for me. I really don't want to be doing this.

9. I don't agree with a decision made by my company management.

10. My company was sold and there is no reason for me to stay. I was not involved or informed of the integration plans, and I don't know where I now fit in.

ANNEX 2

Forms of Non-Salary Compensation

The following are forms of non-salary compensation and should be considered when comparing and evaluating the value of different opportunities:

HEALTH CARE & WELLNESS BENEFITS:

Medical Plan (PPO, HMO, POS, HSA)

Dental Plan

Prescription Plan (typically included with Group Medical Plan)

Mail-in prescription program

Vision Plan

Medical Flexible Spending Account (a mechanism to pay for medical costs with pre-tax dollars)

Long-Term Care Insurance

Employee Assistance Program

Wellness Program

Discounted Gym Membership

On-Site Fitness Center

FINANCIAL BENEFITS:

401(k) Plan

401(k) Employer Match (immediate or deferred vesting?)

Profit Sharing

Retirement Planning or other Financial Advisory Services

Life Insurance (for employee and/or dependents)

Incentive Bonus Plan (How much and what are the conditions?)

Referral Bonus Program (How much and what are the conditions?)

Spot Bonus Program (How much and what are the conditions?)

Educational Assistance

Company Provided Laptop

Company Provided Cell Phone or PDA

Employee Computer Purchase Plan

Auto Insurance

Equity Ownership

Stock Option Plan

Stock Purchase Plan

Cafeteria Type Plan (where you receive cash in lieu of benefits)

LEAVE BENEFITS:

Paid Holidays (How many?)

Paid Jury Duty (How much time?)

Paid Bereavement Leave (How much time?)

Long Term Disability (LTD) (What is the elimination period and coverage amount?)

Short Term Disability (STD) (What is the elimination period and coverage amount?)

Paid Vacation (How much time, how does it accrue, how much is permitted to be carried over to the next year or is it a use it or lose it policy?)

Paid Sick Leave (How many days?)

Paid Military Leave (How many days and do benefits continue during leave?)

Paid Maternity/Paternity (How many days and do benefits continue during leave?)

FAMILY FRIENDLY BENEFITS:

Dependent Care Flexible Spending Account (a mechanism to pay for dependent care (childcare or elderly care) costs with pre-tax dollars)

Paid Family Leave

Flex Time

Telecommuting

On-Site Child Care Facility

OTHER MISCELLANEOUS BENEFITS:

Professional Development

Tuition Assistance

Professional Membership Fees

Casual Days

Pet Health Insurance

Company Sponsored Sports Teams

Company Purchased Tickets for Cultural or Sporting Events

Holiday Parties

Summer Picnic

Performance Awards and Recognition

Concierge Services

ABOUT THE AUTHOR

DANIELLE O. SAUNDERS was the founder and President of Accelligence LLC, a boutique professional services firm which provides strategic, operational, technical and instructional support to the Intelligence Community. Prior to forming Accelligence, Ms. Saunders served as an executive officer of a publicly traded international telecommunications company with revenues in excess of $1 billion, where she implemented and managed corporate governance practices, oversaw standards for all legal, regulatory and exchange listing compliance and participated in private and public debt and capital raising initiatives.

For the first half of her career, Ms. Saunders was in the private practice of law with both Shaw Pittman and Hunton & Williams where she specialized in corporate and securities matters with a focus on corporate governance and debt and capital raising activities.

Ms. Saunders received a Bachelor of Arts in International Affairs degree (Magna Cum Laude) at the George Washington University. She is a graduate of the National Law Center of George Washington University with a J.D. degree with honors. Ms. Saunders lives in Virginia with her husband John and their three children.

www.ingramcontent.com/pod-product-compliance
Lightning Source LLC
Chambersburg PA
CBHW060813280326
41934CB00010B/2677